Around the World
Clothes

Margaret Hall

Heinemann
LIBRARY

www.heinemann/library.co.uk
Visit our website to find out more information about Heinemann Library books.

To order:
☎ Phone 44 (0) 1865 888066
📄 Send a fax to 44 (0) 1865 314091
💻 Visit the Heinemann Library Bookshop at www.heinemann/library.co.uk to browse our catalogue and order online.

First published in Great Britain by Heinemann Library, Halley Court, Jordan Hill, Oxford OX2 8EJ, a division of Reed Educational and Professional Publishing Ltd. Heinemann is a registered trademark of Reed Educational and Professional Publishing Ltd.

OXFORD MELBOURNE AUCKLAND JOHANNESBURG BLANTYRE
GABORONE IBADAN PORTSMOUTH (NH) USA CHICAGO

Designed by Lisa Buckley
Originated by Dot Gradations
Printed in Hong Kong/China

ISBN 0 431 15120 2 (hardback)
06 05 04 03 02
10 9 8 7 6 5 4 3 2 1

British Library Cataloguing in Publication Data
Hall, Margaret
Clothes. - (Around the world)
1.Clothes and dress - Juvenile literature 2.Costume -
I.Title
391

Acknowledgements
The publishers would like to thank the following for permission to reproduce photographs: Michael Scott/Tony Stone, pp. 1, 13; Wolfgang Kaehler, pp. 4a, 14,17, 20, 24; Keren Su/Tony Stone, pp. 4b, 9; Sharon Smith/Bruce Coleman, Inc., p. 4c; Kay Maeritz/Tony Stone, p. 5; BW Stitzer/Photo Edit, p. 6; John Shaw/ Bruce Coleman, Inc., p. 7; Glen Allison/Tony Stone, p. 8; David Hiser/Tony Stone, p. 10; Steve Lehman/Tony Stone, p. 11; JGG/Photo Edit, p. 12; Erica Lansher/Tony Stone, p. 15; Bill Avon/Photo Edit, p. 16; David Young-Wolff/Photo Edit, p. 18; Glen Allison/Tony Stone, p. 19; Wayne Eastep/Tony Stone, p. 21; Kim Saar/Heinemann Library, p. 22; Phil Martin/Heinemann Library, p. 23; Lawrence Migdale/Tony Stone, p. 25; Blaine Harrington III, p. 26; Terry Vine/Tony Stone, p. 27; D. MacDonald/Photo Edit, p. 28; Deborah Davis/Photo Edit, p. 29.

Cover photograph reproduced with permission of Fulvio Eccardi/ECCAR/Bruce Coleman, Inc.

Every effort has been made to contact copyright holders of any material reproduced in this book. Any omissions will be rectified in subsequent printings if notice is given to the publishers.

Any words appearing in the text in bold, **like this**, are explained in the glossary.

Contents

People have needs

People everywhere have the same **needs**. They need food, water and homes. They need to be able to get from place to place. All around the world, people also need clothing.

Where people live makes a difference to what they wear. Some clothing is the same in different parts of the world. Some clothing is different.

Why people need clothing

Clothing **protects** people from heat and cold. It helps them stay comfortable in different kinds of weather.

What people wear sometimes says something about them. It can say something about their **culture**, job or **religion**.

Clothing around the world

All around the world, many people wear clothes that look the same. However, in some places, people wear clothing that is very different.

What people wear depends on the **climate** in the place where they live. It also depends on what they have to make their clothes with.

Clothing in cold places

Some places get very cold. Winters are long, and it snows a lot. People need clothing that **protects** them from the cold.

When people go out in the cold, they wear warm clothes. They cover as much of their bodies as they can.

Cold-weather clothes

Animals that live in cold **climates**, like this llama, have thick coats of **wool** or **fur**. These coats keep the animals warm.

This girl's clothes are made of wool. For thousands of years, people have used wool and fur from animals. They make them into clothing to keep themselves warm.

Clothing in tropical places

Some places have **tropical climates**. The weather is very warm. Sometimes there is a lot of rain.

People need special clothing to **protect** them from the hot sun. They also need clothing that will keep them dry when it rains.

Clothes for tropical weather

In **tropical climates**, it is too warm to wear **wool** or **fur**. People grow plants that have **fibres** used in making cloth. The **cotton** balls in the picture are ready for picking.

Clothes made from plant fibres are light. They are cool to wear and dry quickly when they get wet.

Clothing in deserts

Deserts are very dry places. The days get very hot, but nights can be cold. Strong winds can blow sand all around.

People who live in deserts wear clothing that **protects** them from blowing sand. Their clothing keeps them cool when it is hot and warm when it is cold.

Desert clothing

People who live in **deserts** wear clothing made from **cotton** or **wool**. Cotton is used for cool clothing. Wool is used for warmer clothing.

People wear **robes** and head coverings to **protect** them from the hot sun. Loose clothing lets the air cool the body off, too.

Clothes for safety

People who do dangerous jobs need special clothes to keep them safe. Firefighters need hats, coats and boots that can **protect** them from fire and smoke.

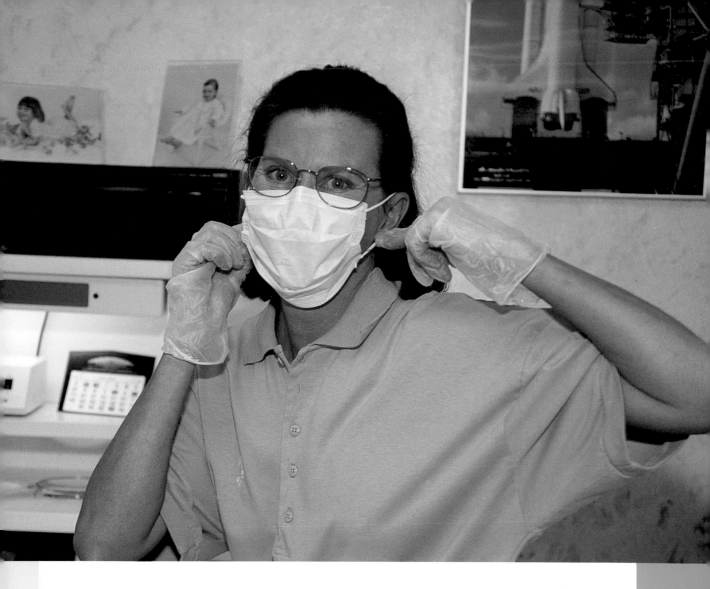

Some workers wear special clothes to keep things clean or to keep **germs** from spreading. That is why a dentist wears a mask and gloves.

Clothes for work

Some people wear special clothes that tell others what their job is. Nurses, police and postal workers wear **uniforms**.

Many people have jobs they do outside.
They may have different uniforms for hot
and cold weather.

City clothes

In large cities around the world, most people wear similar clothes. Office workers often wear suits or dresses.

Most buildings in large cities are heated in the winter and some have **air-conditioning** in the summer. People don't need special clothes when they are inside.

Special clothing

Some people wear special clothing because of their **religion**. Some men may wear special hats. Women may wear long dresses and cover their faces or hair.

In some **cultures**, people wear **traditional** clothing for special days. This clothing often looks like what people of that culture wore long ago.

Photo list

Glossary

air-conditioning way of keeping air cool inside even when it is very hot outside

climate weather in an area throughout the year

cotton plant with fluffy white balls of fibre that are used to make lightweight cloth

culture way of life of a group of people

desert place with a very dry climate

fibre thread-like part of a plant used to make cloth

fur hairy coat of some animals

germ tiny living thing that makes people ill

needs things people must have in order to live

protect keep safe

religion what a person believes about God

robe long, loose piece of clothing

traditional way something has been done or made for a long time

transport ways people move from place to place

tropical place where the weather is hot and rainy

uniform special clothing that shows what a person's job is

wool soft, wavy hair of some animals that can be made into cloth

More books to read

Clothes by Godfrey Hall, Hodder Wayland, 1999

Clothes by Karen Bryant-Mole, Heinemann Library, 1997

Joe Lion's Big Boots by Kara May, Kingfisher, 2000

The Magic Carpet Slippers by Dick King-Smith, Puffin, 2001

Wool by Chris Oxlade, Heinemann Library, 2001

Index

Titles in the *Around the World* series include:

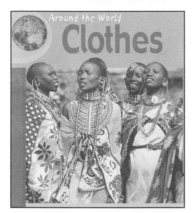

Hardback   0 431 15120 2

Hardback   0 431 15130 X

Hardback   0 431 15121 0

Hardback   0 431 15131 8

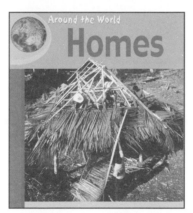

Hardback   0 431 15122 9

Hardback   0 431 15132 6

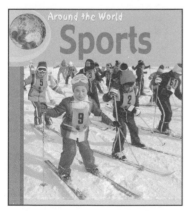

Hardback   0 431 15133 4

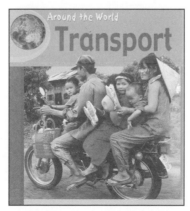

Hardback   0 431 15123 7

Find out about the other titles in this series on our website www.heinemann.co.uk/library